Stacking Winter Wood

Stacking Winter Wood

Poems by

Michael Walls   10-10-2022

For Terry,
        Enjoy's
            Mike

Kelsay Books

Cover photo: © vic_burton (at Flickr)
Author photo: Chris Fox

ISBN: 13-978-1-945752-67-4

Kelsay Books
Aldrich Press
www.kelsaybooks.com

For Erin, Joe, Jack and Fiona.

My heartfelt gratitude to Karen Kelsay for believing in and publishing this book; to Tara Bray, my first poetry writing friend who has read many first drafts and revisions and supported my writing since I started; to Memye Curtis Tucker, my first teacher; to Mary Moore for her insightful assistance with final editing; to Cecilia Woloch and Amy Pence who looked at early drafts of manuscripts that would never have become a book were it not for their advice and encouragement; to the writing group: Jennifer Wheelock, Cathy Carlisi, Beth Gylys, Adrian Fillion, Mickey McConnell and Chelsea Rathburn who provided feedback and helped with revisions for many of the poems in this book and G.G. Najour and the staff at George's who always allowed us to have the big, circular table even though we didn't spend much money and it was the prime spot in the bar; to Ann Ritter for help arranging the order of the poems; and to Diane Shearer, proofreader and mistake-finder extraordinaire. Thank you all.

Contents

III.

IV.

I.

Daybreak

begins with orange light slipping through tree trunks.
Pain, that yesterday, felt like scratching claws
of a cat inside my throat is almost gone. As forsythia
along the driveway starts to take on yellow,
I think how each new spring brings me closer
to a morning when I will wake to a sore throat
or a stomach pain that won't leave until I leave it.

At the theater last night, we watched dancers
offer their bodies to the audience—a woman
lying on her back, her partner with outstretched arms,
hovering over her like a cresting wave, a voice
reciting invocations to God.

The sun pushes aside the fog, and the forsythia
starts to brighten. I consider gods I have known.
The angry, rejected God of my youth who demanded
too much. The God who had no words for my friend,
a physician, when asked by her mother, to explain
to her the true meaning of words like *fatigue,
metastasis.* And finally the god who refuses
to go away, who seems to demand nothing more
than the opportunity to be considered.

The forsythia begins to blaze in the sunlight,
the air we grab so greedily but can never hold,
still visible in the last small patch of fog.

Petroglyphs - Rio Grande Gorge

for Spencer Oedel, 1987-2005

The sun climbs to the top of its arc.
Mountain sheep, morning song birds,
lizards, even the beetles and ants
have disappeared while the gorge
pauses to rest in the heat and quiet,
the only intrusion, the scratch
of sage on denim, crunch of boots
on rocks that once flowed liquid hot.

On a ledge where the trail hangs
above the river, etchings on stone.
Circles that mirror the sun when it rises
over the rim; wavy lines that run
across the face of a rock. I come here,
a day-tripper, to a place where time
is measured by how long it takes to smooth
cuts made in stone; where centuries ago,
someone climbed through cactus, sage,
over jagged rocks to chisel at this spot.

To praise the copper disk that sets
behind the rock, throws shadows
that crawl through millennia in seconds
on the far wall. To honor what shaped the gorge
—the river flowing hundreds of feet below,
the wind that slips down the canyon, stirs
your ashes and fills my tracks with sand.

Climbing Green Mountain

The last hill's the hardest. The bike bucks,
jerks over rocks until at last, I reach the top,
stop where the trail branches toward two valleys,
neither of which I have ridden. Resting
against an oak trunk, I take deep draws
from my water bottle, listen to a barking dog
from a cabin on the next ridge and try to recall

what I was thinking on another afternoon
in the woods behind the house where I grew up.
Now, I can only wonder what a five-year-old
might have thought, how his mysteries
differed from those of a man in his sixties.
I no longer remember what questions he asked
his dog in the quiet of the woods, only that he did.

On a Hot Day

Gatorade slides like an icicle
down my throat. And I
remember a cold Coca-Cola,
years ago, shared behind
my aunt's garage with a friend
of my cousin, an older girl
who already had breasts,
who told me she would like
to screw Steve McQueen
in his red Ferrari and how
I wondered if a Ferrari
had a back seat. The patch
of white that seemed to smile
at me when she lifted
her dress above her knees
sitting cross-legged in the grass.
The way the cold Coke
burned going down.

Blackberry Roads

I spotted them from my truck, around a bend
where ruts formed by runoff make the road slow,
hanging from prickly spines in a scattering of briars.
I picked a handful—choosing only the darkest berries,
purpled black—left the waxy ones still freckled with red.

As a boy, my mother and I picked berries by the bucket.
Then I watched her on broiling summer afternoons,
before a hot stove, her spoon clicking against the pot
while she stirred berries, added sugar, blended
them into a new shape inside the curve of Mason jars.

I drop my harvest into a bowl—dark berries,
picked on a briar-lined road like the ones
my mother and I walked together—cover them
with steaming oatmeal, stir in a dollop of purple jam.
It leaves a trail, like a thread, behind my spoon.

My Father's Leather Jacket

It seemed to burn—the ebony luster
of dark chocolate. It was the first nice coat
he ever owned. For several winters
my father wore it every day. I saw it
tonight in a photograph of James Dean.

And I tried to picture my father
as a rebel with, or without, a cause.
It was the 50's. He was in his mid 20's,
still looked like a teen. I don't recall
him ever mentioning James Dean.

But there was that Saturday afternoon,
when *Gentlemen Prefer Blondes* played
at the Royal Theater. He kept talking
about how Jane Russell was stacked.
My mother put on "Day-O", cranked up
the volume, then dropped the album cover

—Harry Belafonte, open-shirted—on the table.
The slammed door echoed through the house.
There was a swagger I had never before seen,
never saw again as he walked to the car,
his leather jacket slung over his shoulder.

Pokeweed

Tired, I slow my run to a stop beside the lake,
by a head-tall stand of them. New berries,
hard and white, clumped in upward-pointing clusters.
Leaves that wear the pale green of early summer,
like the tender young ones my grandmother
gathered each spring, before they turned toxic,
fried in bacon grease to a *mess of poke sallit
to purify the system.* Vein-like streaks, the color
of diluted blood, runs up stems carrying pigment
to darken berries, that in the fall, will droop
in poisonous plumpness like the ones I swallowed
as a child too young to remember, when my parents
rushed me to the hospital to have my stomach pumped.

In my earliest memory, I'm lying on my father's bare chest,
wanting my mother, and crying. He was trying
to comfort me. He may have told me what I now know:
that my mother was away because her sister died,
then at the hospital where my sister was born.
Was that when I first heard of birth and death?
What I remember is this: He told me my sister's name
was Becky. I asked him if his nipples were pokeberries.

A Fall Day

Sun glints off blinds
blazing streaks
across hospital walls.
Through the window, hills
splashed with October
roll toward blue mountains.
Mist from an unseen jet
leaves a trail, flimsy and white,
across a cloudless sky.

For a moment, a boy hangs
suspended from a leafless limb,
drops silently to the ground,
disappears beneath a pile
of yellow leaves.

Waking in a Cabin in the Woods

Rain strikes metal flashing around the chimney.
Light starts to seep through the trees.
Leaves tremble under the pelt of drops.

When I was a boy, I would listen in bed,
as birds chattered and cawd, then gave way
to the crackle of frying bacon, the *palump*
palump of perking coffee. And I would
wonder where the birds went during the day.

Later, it was my time to get up first.
To the stirs of a waking city, I brewed
the coffee, made school lunches,
watched houses empty into the street,
listened to slapping tires turn to steady drone.

Now, the age of my parents when the cancer
came that killed them, I watch a spider
crawl across the circle formed by my lamp.
A cobweb, sways in the shadows.

Robert Joffrey's Coat

It is easy to imagine the owner wearing it
on a chilly fall walk through Greenwich Village
near the dance studio. A classic design
in gray herringbone, *Simpson-tailored*
for Simpson-Piccadilly. Made in London.

Perhaps he saw ballets in the swaying limbs
of trees in Washington Square Park.
Perhaps leaves flickering on the ground
around the trunks reminded his tired feet
of their tap dancing youth in Seattle.

After his death, it hung for months
in the dance studio until his friend gave
the coat to my daughter, Erin: a new student
who wore an unlined Army field jacket
her first winter in New York.

Winters later, the years have erased
his scent from its fabric. Dry cleaning
and rain have long since taken away
the last residue of his hair, his skin.

His company left New York, became
Joffrey Ballet of Chicago. On the platform
at the Times Square station, bundled
against winter in Robert Joffrey's coat,
Erin waits for the No. 1 train.

II.

Mandelstam

(1891 - 1938?)

The poet's life closed behind him as the dark
Siberian winter dropped into the camp,
his only comfort, the ragged yellow coat
he wore the day the Cheka came to take him.

(Nadia's package was returned: *addressee is dead*
said the girl behind the post office counter.)
His poems, handwritten notes, sallowed by age,
hidden by Nadia in a half-filled straw basket,
were dispersed among friends he never knew,
buried under the black snow of Stalin winter.

Nadia kept his verses to her death, mumbled them
at night to the spinning machine in the textile factory
where no one could hear, recited them softly
to winds that blew across the steppes
as she trudged the rutted streets of a dozen
Russian villages, herself an exiled nomad
who would never return to live again in Moscow.

When the black snow thawed, other writers emerged,
Akhmatova, Pasternak, Solzhenitsyn—rehabilitated.
No one can reclaim the muted dead.

Hiking to Slaughter Gap - November, 2002

The trail connects two peaks, separated
by holy ground where Creeks and Cherokees
fought. Red and gold treetops clothe the gap
as autumn seems to strut through the ridges
and hillsides. Bare trunks stand like a line
of soldiers along the hip of Blood Mountain

and pull me back to a world I came to the woods
to escape. A world that waits—while generals
prepare for a war my mind wrestles to understand,
my sleep filled with images—corpses lying
on hot desert sand, women in shrouds,
pressed palms held against their breasts.

At a switchback where granite outcrops
and thick undergrowth crowd the trail,
I lose the path, break through a spider's web.
It dangles from a limb like torn lace,
holds a leaf, floating and twisting in midair.

Pantoum for Fallujah

White phosphorous, our troops call *Willie Pete,*
napalm mixed with jet fuel.
It burns the skin, only clothes survive.
They claimed it was used to illuminate.

Napalm mixed with jet fuel
turns the night sky white.
They claimed it was used to illuminate
a city softened by *shock and awe.*

It turns the night sky white,
but this time we used it in daylight.
The city softened by *shock and awe*;
the operation named *shake and bake.*

This time we used it in daylight,
death clouds creeping through town.
The operation named *shake and bake*
left children charred, their clothes intact.

Death clouds creeping through town,
we left Fallujah in ruins,
children charred, their clothes intact.
Hummers rolled east, back to Baghdad.

We left Fallujah in ruins
a cradle of civilization called Babylon.
Hummers rolled east, back to Baghdad.
Open Sesame, den of forty thieves.

In a cradle of civilization called Babylon,
it burns the skin, only clothes survive.
Open Sesame, den of forty thieves,
white phosphorous, our troops call *Willie Pete.*

25

The Drone Pilot

You can't get what night shift's really like
'til you've worked it. Fighting to stay awake,
finally getting off and there's this piss-yellow strip
of light just appearing there on top of the parking lot
telling you it's already tomorrow. Believe me,
they don't call it graveyard shift for nothing.
Same computer screen every night. Trailing
the same dude around the same desert mountains,
raggedy-ass little towns—a long way from Vegas,
man—fingers burning from too hot coffee
in a too thin cup. Last night, I got special orders.

I was waitin'—timings gotta be just right,
when he's someplace off from everybody else.
Right then, my fingers slipped on the coffee cup.
Thought I'd scalded my damn dick off.
Almost didn't catch him when he stepped out
of the car. Just before it hit, something small
came running up. At first, I thought it might be
a kid, but my photographer claimed it was a dog.
Then all that extra paper work. Kept me late.
Now the sun's way up in the sky. Not much time
to grab any extra sleep today. Gotta pick up
Amanda and Jason from soccer at 4:00.

Independence Day

On the back of a wheelchair,
a flag and a rumpled piece of cardboard.
Black letters, "Homeless Veteran."
A line of cars maneuver past
into the Kroger parking lot.

Inside—wines, cheeses, breads
stacked to eye level, a tank
where red-coated lobsters slide
from side to side. "Born in the USA"
floats through the aisles, its edge
smoothed by the sound system,
its anger stolen by time.

I choose a chardonnay, baguettes,
a cheese ball for the picnic
in the park, where fireworks will fill
the night with booms and we'll all sing
when the band plays "This Land
is your Land", watch lights—red, white,
and blue—explode across the sky, float
back to the ground like spent stars.

Oppenheimer

Big drops—cold even in August—
splatter dust on the high mesa,
form rivulets in shallow arroyos.
To the southwest, clouds hang
from the top of a mountain ridge.
On the other side lies Los Alamos.

I shiver in the cold rain. Wonder,
if he ever shivered that summer?
Perhaps at the perfect beauty
of a mathematical equation? Or maybe
the brilliance, never before witnessed,
of the test blast that turned night
to light? His aloneness, facing
the glow of the day's last cigarette?

Plateau du Vercors

The trail twists beside a waterfall,
barely a trickle in late summer.
At the crest, an hour's climb, the path
flattens to rocky grassland,
hillocks dotted with stunted trees.
Twin caves stare from a hill,
watching over the narrow path.

But the Germans came in gliders,
landed behind the hill, silent
as the night wind. A shepherd tried
to warn the fighters in the caves.
A bent metal cross, brown with rust
marks the spot where the Nazis
killed him. Twenty-eight resisters
fled the caves in the night.
Seventeen reached the valley.

The trail ends at a stone wall
carved with names.
GUIGUES AMORE - 22 ANS,
MOSCONE JEAN - 19 ANS,
BOUCARD XAVIER - 44 ANS,
NICOLAS GASTON - 23 ANS,
ALGOUD ALBERT - 37 ANS,
KAUFFMANN MARIAL - 37 ANS,
GALLAND GILBERT - 21 ANS,
SIMIAND RENE - 23 ANS.
Tombes en heros pour France libre.

Almost seventy years since that night
rattled with machine gun fire, flowers
grow beside graves. Delicate blue gentians,
protected by law, bloom in patches
next to half-buried mortar fragments.
Evening shadows spread across the trail.
A shepherd and her dog bring a flock
of sheep to drink at the creek.

Cajones

The local radio station jars me awake.
No balls! Politicians don't have the balls
to deal with the wetbacks. Outside,
morning bells from the Catholic Church,
peal through this California wine town—
like the Baptist bells in the Georgia town
I knew as a child, chiming each evening
reminding timeless little separate
but equal boys to go home for supper.

In the afternoon, a happier bell clangs
from the train that ferries tourists, red-faced
from Cabernet, through the wine country.
They watch workers in the vineyards.
Workers with names like Ramone, Jose,
Maria and Marta, who came north
to valleys named Sonoma and San Joaquin.
Workers whose soft brown fingers,
unlike machines, won't bruise the grapes.

Hard Rain

Friday morning. Downward looking men
who wear baseball caps, orange vests
against brown skin, descend on McGill Place
Condominiums—mowing, weeding, blowing leaves.
Each time I pass them, hear the music
of their talk, I wish again I could understand,
could listen to their stories—the dirt roads
they left in Chiapas or Mazatenango, the routes
they took to come here where they keep
the flowers blooming outside my building.
Did they wade the river? Did they cross
the desert at a place where laws make criminals
of people who leave them water? Today,
we stand together beneath a stairway,
pouring rain only inches from our faces.
I wait for a break to make a run to my car.
They take a break from the heat. Only one, thin
as the leaf blower cocked on his hip, returns
a timid smile. *Mucho aqua. Si, mucho agua.*

On a Silent Morning

When we rose up in arms at dawn of 1994 . . . we did it
Simply to be heard, to say 'we are here.'
                                        —Subcommandante Marcos

Light diffuses through my kitchen window.
The bulk on the table lightens, takes shape
as spun clay filled with Mexican sunflowers
shipped north for my winter pleasure.
The morning news is about the falling peso.
Banks are nervous—no mention of the rape
of Cecilia Rodriguez, who spoke for the Zapatistas.
I picture the sun's unifying light starting
to peep around corners, creep down canyons
on Wall Street where the Mexican President
delivered a check borrowed from the swollen
bellies of children. In another hour, that sunlight
will stalk through heavy air in Chiapas,
warm corpses that lie in dew by the roadside,
give a dull sheen to sweat on blue steel.

A Labor Arbitration

She worked at a nuclear power plant.
She was fired for lying.
She lied about why
She had missed work.
She said she told her foreman
She had jury duty, instead of that
She had had a miscarriage.
She testified that
She tried for five years to get pregnant.
She was afraid people would believe, as
She believed, that
She was not adequate as a wife.
She was afraid that if
She told her foreman

He would tell others.
He said nuclear workers must be trustworthy.
He testified that
He had no choice.
He had to fire her because
He couldn't trust someone who lied to
Him.

Whose Woods

Treeless top of an unnamed peak,
cleared years ago for helicopters, so soldiers
could practice combat landings in a forest.
Now abandoned to thorny brush,
flowering milkweed, favored by monarchs.
A good place to pause after a hard climb.

The woods are quiet but for the buzz
of cicadas conducting their ritual search
for a mate. A thrashing erupts from the top
of a tree beyond my sight. While I listen
to screams, some animal learns how to die.
For long moments, the forest is silent.
At last, cicadas resume their search.
A raccoon rustles the brush, runs down
a ravine, blood on its face.

Reclamation

A maze of rusted pipes and conveyors, weathered buildings,
mounds of bare dirt, fill the space between Copperhill
and Ducktown. A chemical plant with good Union jobs, that left.
Now there's a new owner, new product—"organic" chemicals.
New cars sit on tracks reclaimed from stray dogs, but
the same red stream runs from the bowels of the plant
to the Ocoee River. On Brush Creek Trail—near where rafters
run the rapids, hardwoods end abruptly in hills once stripped
to desert by poison spat from a smelter in Ducktown—later
reclaimed with pine trees that now lie where they fell—
killed by beetles that no longer sleep in winter.
A box turtle, strayed from the hardwoods, head and feet
tucked inside its shell, hides in plain sight on leafless ground.

Incan Forest

We twisted North, across the equator,
on the Pan Am Highway, through rocky
desert mountains—sparse brush,
wind-bent mesquites—nearly naked
slopes scarred by haphazard gullies.

The driver, a bearded Brit, came
to work Amazon Basin oil fields,
married a local woman, bought a bar,
never missed Liverpool a bloody bit.
He remembers lush mountains, denuded,
forests turned to lumber and exported. Now,
it's too arid for hardwoods to come back.

At a street market in a dusty village
high in the Andes, I bought a blanket.
Unlike the blankets in Quito's shops—
tight-woven pictorials of animals
and Indian life—it had straight-lined designs
in bold colors—loosely stitched
wispy-thin white thread, its softness
broken by burrs and thistles that hitched
to sheep grazing barren hillsides.
Blended bands of grays, blues, brown.
Raw and drab, like the mountains.

Ponce de Leon Avenue - circa 2002

It wears winter like a shroud. From Grace
Methodist to Druid Hills Baptist Church,
like God's alley, it forms a gauntlet
for Atlanta's damned. Once, Ponce
had a ball park with a magnolia tree
in deep center field, an ivy-clad bank
in right, where The Babe hit a home run.

The hope is the new mall: Whole Foods
where center field used to be, Home Depot
instead of home plate. For now, cars still rent
for "$8.88 a d y (some con itions ap ly),"
in the lot beside Lou's Blues Bar.
In Clermont Lounge, oldest strip joint in town,
Blondie recites her poetry while crushing
Pabst Blue Ribbon cans between her breasts.

Behind the new Staples, roofless men
stand beneath the magnolia, hands cupped
around cigarettes, dripping from rain.
Further up the hill, a lone man in a baseball cap
that says "Atlanta – Olympic City," shuffles
past a long-haired girl with darting eyes
and a needle, who kneels in knee-deep kudzu
behind a refrigerator that has no door.

Transition Neighborhood

Just four blocks away, a fourteen-lane gash of asphalt
cleaves the city; and it's only a ten-minute walk

to the tallest building in the Southeast. Yet,
for months, in the quiet just before night

turns to day, I would hear the questioning
who, who of an owl—always from the direction

of several blocks that separate gated condos
from Whole Foods, where johns still cruise,

junkies talk to themselves and curse
at strangers. I looked hard, but never found

where the owl stayed, never knew if it
was a pioneer testing its luck in the city

with new digs in one of the Bradford pears
planted by developers beside the tennis courts

or an old timer, holding on in a gnarly oak
in the park where homeless people sleep.

III.

A Drop

of sweat, soaked in salt and sunscreen,
slips down my forehead to cool me,

a dribble that's traveled for aeons,
from silent pools deep in the earth

to the farthest edge of the ether and back,
emerging and re-emerging—as clouds,

fog, rain and flakes that filled up woods
with snow. Once, it poured crimson

from a hole in the side of a soldier, soothed
the parched lips of a killer, plunged

in white torrents through canyon walls, filled
an apple as it darkened at the close of summer,

lodged in the lungs of a shipwrecked sailor,
threw spectrums of color across the sky.

It swelled a tumor in a dying woman's brain.
It was a timeless workhorse that helped ferry

gold-seeking plunderers, turned turbines
to run factories, cranked gears to grind grain.

It's risen from cooling towers in vaporous ghosts,
gathered in droplets on wires that carry power

to heat homes, light schools and plants
that make missiles. It launched sperm,

floated fetuses, formed mud that speckled
the legs of children playing in the park. It's been

wine, poison, piss, tears and mother's milk
before it came to me in a sip, or perhaps the kiss

of a lover, before it became part of me,
before it slides from my skin to the dirt.

Chama

Some say, in the language of the Tewa,
Chama means *here they wrestled.*
Others, that it's from their word for *red*,
like the dirt they turned into pottery,
the river that carved their valley.

We came there when February flirted
with April. Magpies with no ground
to peck, perched—shiny as lumps
of waxed coal—on fence posts.
Snow lay a foot deep. Drifts turned wet
in glaring sunlight. But, after dark,
clouds rolled down from the mountains,
turned the night cold. Coyotes howled.

In the morning, their red-tinged tracks
dotted the snow along the river bank.

Heat Wave

It's a hundred and four and humid.
For weeks, the news has been the same:
local lakes turn to mudflats, the West,
burning in a scorched patchwork
of smoke and out-of-control wildfires.

Impatiens drop like weighted feathers
from wilted stems. Crepe myrtles
droop lower and lower. Each day
more rain refuses to fall. At the close
of each day, a blood orange sun pauses
atop the Bank of America Tower, slides
down the building's back, abandons
the city to the night, hurting and hot.

Night Storm

After midnight, rain slants through the orb
of the floodlight. I watch it, remembering
the dry underbrush we saw yesterday—sickly
as the faces in the ER on a Saturday night,
where everyone has a bad weekend. Envision
it coming alive as drops burrow their way
down to thirsty roots. Imagine the creek bed,
where yesterday, our boots left dusty prints,
filling bank to bank, and the red clay skin
that surrounds the lake shrinking an inch
or two. I wonder if more rain will fall, content
for now, to listen to an unexpected break
in a long drought and marvel at our mother
reasserting herself with tattoos on the roof.

Labor Day - 2005

Clouds intermittently erase the sun
from my porch. A blue-tail skink moves
back and forth, looking for warm spots.
From time to time, a rooster crows
down in the valley. Otherwise, it's quiet.

Earlier this morning, a neighbor I don't
often see, dropped in to say hello.
We drank coffee, talked in soft voices.
In the background, Yo-Yo Ma and news
of Katrina alternated on the radio.

When the levees broke in Louisiana,
cottonmouths swam among corpses
in the streets. People, locked in shelters,
huddled in terror while butterflies
flitted on patches of high ground.

A fast-moving cloud sweeps the porch
and lightens the floor. The skink
braces on its front legs, faces the sun,
its pulsing neck bent upward
like the delicate curve of a cello.

The Last Frontier

for my father

I

For years, we talked about driving—
unhurried—to Alaska. But I was busy.
Now I'm riding down Kenai Peninsula
in a Homer Stage Line van—fourteen years
overdue. And everything reminds me
of you—corkscrew braids of the woman
asleep on the seat in front of me, twisted
like your body those last days, when I held
a cup of water to your lips and it was all
you could do to say *yes.*

II

On the day I was born, you were not yet
twenty-one, at home in Georgia
while friends and brothers were off at war.
When you saw me, you said I was ugly,
and my mother cried. I wonder if you stayed
up late that night? If you read letters
from Italy, France, islands in the Pacific
and cursed the foot that made you 4-F,
kept you home to make your wife cry?

III

In June, water comes to the edge of Route 1
south of Anchorage, marshes formed
by runoff snow on one side, on the other
the ocean. Distant rows of peaks hold back
the world. Past a stand of beetle-battered
spruce trees between Ninilchik and Anchor Point,
the road dips to cross a creek. Just before
the lowest point, a road sign warns, *BUMP.*

IV

Depression child, your life began in a look-alike
company house—red-dirt yard—cotton mill village,
where fathers retired with a gold watch
and a cough. At seven, you almost died
from blood poison; learned to smoke cigarettes.
You raised five kids. In summer, you took us all
to Daytona. You fished. Drove on the beach.

V

In midnight dusk, bars and galleries
along Pioneer Avenue appear
as shadowy outlines. Like we seemed
sometimes to each other. Bound
by blood, love of baseball. Split
by politics. We knew what to protect,
hidden like keepsakes in locked boxes.

VI

The captain maneuvers the boat to a spot
near a raft of sea lions and cuts the engine.
A hawk hovers overhead, ready to snatch up
leftover pieces of halibut. Waves lap
the bottom of the boat. We bob
on the water and wait for the feeding.

VII

Clouds hang low over Kachemak Bay.
On the beach, pickup trucks sling dirt
into wind that carries it out of sight. Rain
stings my face, drives me into a café
where they play the country music
you loved—"I'm so Lonesome, I Could Cry"—
and the chowder is thick as the clouds.

50

A Late Spring in Blue Ridge

The cashier places a weight on the scale.
The needle falls, moves back up
as she drops chocolates into the tray.
When it points straight up, she empties
them into a bag, takes my money. I head
down Depot Street—past missing jonquils,
oak trees that poke naked limbs
at cold March wind. Snow swirls again
in north Georgia, hiking trails a mass
of mud and packed ice, in this longest,
coldest winter anyone can remember.
My neighbor's take: *Shows what a crock
of shit all that global warming talk is.*

Dark chocolate spreads tropical warmth
through my body. I read that ski runs
in Canada are brown. Wonder what they say
about climate change around the mailbox
in Vancouver. Hold back the last bonbon
for tomorrow. The cat huddles under a blanket,
her body already shedding its winter coat.

Shadows

Slogging through shimmer
radiating off hot asphalt
down a dog day sidewalk
thankful for the swath of shadow
thrown by the thirsty arms
of a magnolia tree.
Scentless blooms. Ocher
of old parchment tinged brown
at the edges.

Forty years since the night
those branches shielded
my rain-splattered Plymouth
windows fogged
"Strangers in the Night"
drifting from the radio
thick red hair
dripping blossoms
under the street light
the scent of shalimar
petals falling.

A-Tisket a-Tasket

Once, we stepped through a sagging gate
into a garden. The party went on without us
while we walked amid fronds of maidenhair
and moss, Ella singing in the background.
Your shoulder brushed my arm; I felt summer
on your skin, imagined its salt on my tongue.
With pocketed hands, I watched water ripple
over a rock like a ghost in the moonlight.

On the day tiger lilies are starting to slump,
I'm driving a pick-up truck through the mountains.
Rain hides the white line, rattles the roof,
blurs a voice on the radio from years ago,
and I'm recalling that next morning

toast and crumbly cheese, the way
you balanced your coffee cup on finger tips
—prayer-like—while you blew away the steam.
I can no longer remember those words,
the last ones before you stopped
mid-sentence, and stared out the window,
before *I don't want to talk anymore.*

Slinging a Stone

I choose a good one, smooth, flat, curved
just right—perfect fit inside the crescent
between my thumb and forefinger.
A bend in the knee, a sidearm sling,
quick snap of the wrist for the speed
it needs to get a good first bounce.
A decent hit off the top of a wave
could get five—maybe even six—hops,
a slap on the water for each stone
you flung at me that I couldn't dodge.
It sails just off the water, touches
down in a trough and sinks.

Glory Bound

Cold rain bites at my face. Where two trails meet,
a young man falls in behind me. Mud-spattered Nikes,
no hat, no gloves. *I raise horses, lead rides to make*
ends meet. Mainly though, what I do is preach
the gospel. We round a bend, head into a head wind.
I pull my hood closer. *I use to be an atheist. But that*
left me restless. Like this storm. 'Til I found Jesus.

Politely, he asks if he can ask, if I'm saved. Politely,
I tell him that's a complicated question and anyway,
it's private. *No problem.* We walk on. He talks on.
I grew up in Kansas. My wife—she's from Texas.
And she preaches the gospel too. We're building
our dream house on a piece of land across the line,
in Tennessee. Right now, we rent. No kids, yet.

At the trailhead, we say goodbye, climb into our trucks.
He backs up, pulls back in, gets out—engine running—
walks over to my window, shivering, water running
down his red face: *Sir, I'd just like to say one thing:*
Jesus is the way. If I die tonight, I know for sure
where I'll be tomorrow morning.

55

Erosion

After making love, we lie apart,
no longer with expectation, watch
a moth bounce against the window,
trying to return to the world it knows.
Later, at high tide, we walk down
the beach to a spot where the shore
stops at a line of trees—bleached, leafless,
but still standing. A watery wasteland
undulates among toppled live oaks,
Medusa roots drying in the sun.
Momentary tracks left by shore birds
fade back into gray sand. A wave climbs
over a clump of dry dirt and swallows it.

One Year

My words remained in my throat like small animals
clawing at a clogged passageway. Meanwhile
summer turned city streets to a hot griddle,
skyscrapers stood defiant in the daily haze.

The sun burned late into autumn. Streams
dried to dust. Fall foliage blazed red
while mountaintops became islands
in a sea of gray smoke from forest fires.

Rain and snow finally came in December.
In January, Flat Creek froze so thick I could walk
on it, my boots inches above its diminished flow
that pushed on toward the Toccoa River.

Today you called. We exchanged *are you okays*.
I told you about the daffodil that emerged yesterday
like a bird peeking from its nest, now frozen in place
by last night's surprise spring ice storm.

IV.

The Bridge

Beyond the hanging concrete, furious sheets of rain and wind make this swath of interstate impenetrable. Like Fagin's boys, we're the lucky ones to have refuge: me, in my sad pickup truck loaded with soaked furniture rescued from Saturday morning yard sales; a young woman in a leather-seated red Miata, her tanned skin, the smoothness of butterscotch pudding, wearing a starched white shirt, blue and red lettering, *Ole Miss - Delta, Delta, Delta;* and a middle-aged guy on a Harley, American flag do-rag drawn across beaded forehead, sleeveless black shirt and tobacco-stained teeth. We sit on a guardrail splattered with tar and bird shit, listen to her CD player, each surprised the others like Carlos Santana. Like a scene from a black and white movie, he leans forward, offers a cigarette, then a cup-hand light. She accepts both. They tease me that the rain has turned the mattress on my truck into a homemade water bed. We giggle, punch each other like school kids. The downpour retreats and semis start to roll again.

The Commerce Comet

His face, barely recognizable, stared
from the TV screen, no longer
the blond slugger whose muscles
once rippled and rose beneath pinstripes
like ridges in the Oklahoma mining town
where his father taught him to hit
a curveball. The familiar face, tanned,
always grinning, now narrow and stark,
dark lines where jaws pulled inward.
Wispy hair hung above oversized ears.
The news man called it the most savage cancer
his doctors had ever seen. Callers
on talk radio complained that drunks
did not deserve new livers. And I recalled

my father, a teetotaler most of his life,
on a rainy Sunday afternoon
in rumpled pajamas, two-day beard,
coiled plastic tube running in and out
his sallow skin—watching one more
ball game on television and talking
baseball; that dog day afternoon, 1951,
Mickey Mantle and Joltin' Joe
playing in the same outfield; the night
at Griffith Field when he and I watched
Mantle stroke his one thousandth base hit.
The entire stadium rose as he trotted
to the dugout. The Mick stopped,
stood on the top step, and tipped his cap.

The Blues Singer

The hat and heels are red,
separated by a clinging black dress.
She mops drops of sweat
from beneath dark glasses.
Twin loops of plastic pearls,
white hot as the spotlight,
slide apart with each curl
of her shoulders around the mic.
One loop tightens like a choke hold,
the other becomes a dancing
semi-circle that glides
across a black V. A low sound,
the texture of river sand, rises
from where the pain lives
I been down . . . .

Settlement

I

They sit across a table in a house that's for sale,
drink coffee from china cups they once chose
together. Between silences, they pass
a yellow pad back and forth, take turns
placing lines and squiggles on the page.
When all the figures are down, they sit back
in their chairs. She fingers a chain he once
clasped around her neck. For just a moment,
he places his hand casually on her arm.

II

It's the smaller details that linger like a scent
remains on clothes worn seasons ago:
the day he returned from the Keys, sunburned feet
lined with white stripes to match his flip-flops;
warmth she felt, like the flush from a glass of wine
when a smile undressed his face; the memory
of a strand of hair when she makes the bed.

III

He gave the book of Shakespeare's sonnets
to a friend, the shirt from Mexico to Goodwill,
moved the watercolor into a room he seldom
enters. Today, the lamp beside the bed
became the latest casualty. The switch that had
to be so carefully clicked to just the right spot
stopped clicking at all. The only thing left
she would recognize is a sweater
that no longer wears the scent of perfume.

Carmel-by-the-Sea - 8:07 P.M.

I took with me certain simple criteria . . . that
which made for more life . . . was good;
which made for less life was bad.
                                        —Jack London

A hill of crystalline sand curves
around the beach like an amphitheater.
At center stage, where Jack London
must have walked, soundless watchers
clump around bonfires and wait. The sun,
a shimmering plate hovers on a pastel wall.
Children sling plastic frisbees through air
moist and chilled like the coming night.

Shadows lengthen across blanched earth.
The sun quickens its descent as if snipped
from an invisible string. Then exactly
one thousand, four hundred
and forty-one minutes since it last slid
below the same horizon, that proletarian
star drops beneath the wave tops.

A Snake Skin

splotched to match dead leaves,
shriveled and cracked like parchment,
lies discarded on my front porch.
Only the underbelly, toughened
from sliding through spring mud,
over rocks and adobe-hard dirt
in summer drought, remains intact.

Unable to hide on the swept floor
it lies stretched out in front
of the crack where the screen
doesn't quite meet the frame,
as if, its owner, having outgrown
its way of being in the world,
shucked its identity, its scars,
and checked them at the door.

Meals on Wheels

Got nobody left 'cept my cousin Clara.
But Clara don't live too close.
Her socks shush on pine planks
as she walks through the orange glow
from a space heater that reflects off
young faces in old frames. Another strand,
like the shriveled body of the man
down the street, curled, fetus-like
between rails on a hospital bed, eyes
opening as he whispers *God bless you*
when I touch his arm; the faces
I once knew that appear then recede
in his. Together, they form a thread.
Connect me to the unease of life
post-middle age. I clasp her hands
as I leave, heed her warning to *watch out*
going down those old porch steps.

Trips

A Texas two lane, long as wine-stretched
speeches at a retirement party, finally ends.
Fifties-style motel, plastic cups, the color
of rain clouds, stacked on the sink, couple
in the next room, drunk, singing at 2:00 a.m.
And "Glory Days" sounds too familiar.

For years, I kept an old x-ray of my foot.
Broken metatarsal, a vacant space no wider
than a needle, shadowy Terra del Fuego
no longer attached to the mainland.

In Santa Fe, I think I see an old lover
at a bus stop, miles and years from the city
where I last saw her. I brake hard.
But a U-Haul truck passes between us.

I drive on while re-runs creep up
in stutter steps. Wonder what's up ahead;
if it's like after midnight in a blues bar
where encores go on and on, but
"The Thrill Is Gone" is not just a song.

Sunday Morning - after the Argument

Twin stains, like bloodshot eyes, stare
upward from the bottom of stemmed glasses
left on the coffee table. Beneath the whirling fan,
The New Yorker cover flutters indifferently
like the wave you give your neighbor
when you step outside to get the newspaper.
Radar spots pulse across the Weather Channel.
A thin light slants through the kitchen window
onto a mortgage coupon—a week
overdue. A half-burnt candle stands
on the window ledge, rounded rim folding in
toward a crater that smells like lilac.

Old Hippies Come to Happy Hour

It's a place where turquoised tourists
thank God it's Friday with martinis
and elk burgers. But up by the band,
sit an aging hippie and his old lady,
matching gray ponytails, faces
deep-lined by unforgiving desert sun.
No words pass between them,
as if fifty years on the mesa,
off the grid, leave little else to say.
They alone, lower their heads
when the band closes with "The Weight,"
a tribute to Levon Helm. As the band
disassembles, the man's stiff fingers
struggle to count out his change, then they
shuffle to the door, unnoticed except
to a peer who would have envied them
years ago and might still. Out on the street
waits a rusted out truck, caked with dust.

Keeping Count

The days of our years are three score and ten
and if by reason of strength they have four score years
yet is their strength, labor and sorrow
for it is soon cut off, and we fly away.
                        —Psalms 90:10

I.

Triple digits. Second day in a row.
Out on the highway, late summer corn
that stands barely three-feet high,
hasn't seen water in three weeks.
On the patio, black-eyed susans,
petals curled at the tip, slouch
down the sides of baskets.

II

The summer I was fifteen:
Patchy grass in right field,
running hard. Line drive hooks
just past my fingers, lands
in a puff of white chalk.

III

The lawn hangs on with two waterings
a week, fading from green, to yellow,
to brown. I bring in some stems,
trim them on a slant, place them in a vase.

IV

The summer I was eighteen:
Under a pier, past midnight,
a blanket, a six-pack,
two late bloomers play catch up.

V

The sun dives in and out behind
high-flying clouds. Branch tips
scratch at the window pane. I lace up,
stretch, slather on sunscreen,
head out for a jog before the storm.

VI

Summer 1994: Szentendre,
hot afternoon, cold beer, strange voices
thick from palinka, Bob Seger singing
"That Old Time Rock and Roll"
on a boom box. A small, gray bird
lights on my table, hops so close
its wings leave a chill on my hand.

VII

I buy some wood—off the waste pile—
at a discount from a Vietnam vet,
three years my senior, still making
a living *wrasslin' with firewood.*
Beat up old truck groans from the load
going home to the other end of the county.

Stoop, lift, bend. Cradle each log
between logs from the row below.
Stack winter wood on the back porch.

At a Kitchen Table

he eats spotted cheese and bread, sips tea.
Outside, cherry blossoms pile up. Crows
peck in the dirt. His canvases surround us,
buttes layered in shades of red, pintos
beside a pasture gate, saw-toothed mountains
flecked with snow. But, today, as he talks,

he paints a self-portrait: a man searching
for black and white. The wife, kids,
left when he came to the desert to paint.
His second wife, like him, now sick
with cancer. The way he wonders
if he's selfish to want to be the first to go.

Lately, on Sundays when rates are low,
he makes calls to grandchildren
he doesn't know. A pair of crows
burst from a copse of cottonwoods,
streak across the sky. The wind picks up.
Blossoms rush past the window.

Keeping Faith

As a boy, he glimpsed the spirit once,
maybe twice, but never felt the tearful,
pew-gripping call the preacher talked about.
Now, taxiing down a fog-covered runway,
he has trouble defining the time he felt
closest to God, considers the instant
he first touched the face of his child, still moist
from birth, or a morning on a mountain ledge
watching soundless breezes ruffle patches
of Alpine flowers, the quiet broken only
by rocks he threw down to the ice below.
These are the moments he recalls as he looks
through icy rain at a man in a bucket truck,
spewing chemicals from a spray gun
to strip icy stalactites from the wing
of a Boeing 757. Later, from 30,000 feet,
he'll watch fire devour a forest. Black smoke
that rises like a jagged mountain, then
turns gray as it trails to a windblown wisp.
Now, shrouded beneath a yellow hood
is a face he looks into, and wants to trust.

Nothing Much

is happening at the Holiday Inn lounge:
one drinker at the bar, silently sliding
fingers up and down the smooth sides
of a highball glass. The bartender nods.
Need another one? The man's eyes
turn from the mirror-slick surface of the bar
to the baseball game on the muted TV.
Yeah, why not? You know those tests
I told you about? Well, they came back
positive. The waitress moves around
the room in a slow triangle, from the bar,
to the jukebox, to the couple drinking
Coronas in the corner. Hiss and crackle
from whiskey splashed on ice cubes echoes
through the silence. The bartender sets
a new glass on a clean napkin, pushes back
the credit card. *It's on me.* The jukebox
plays "Jumping Jack Flash". The Braves
nip the Dodgers in the bottom of the ninth.

Acknowledgments

Grateful acknowledgement and appreciation to the editors of the following journals and magazines where some of these poems first appeared, sometimes in slightly different forms or different titles.

Atlanta Review: "Keeping Faith"
Bayou Magazine: "My Father's Leather Jacket"
Calamaro: "Pokeweed"
The Chattahoochee Review: "Plateau du Vercors" and "Ponce de Leon Avenue – circa 2002"
Chiron Review: "Nothing Much" and "Robert Joffrey's Coat"
Coffeehouse: "A Fall Morning"
Cold Mountain Review: "On a Silent Morning"
The Comstock Review: "A Snake Skin"
Common Ground Review: "Glory Bound"
Cumberland Poetry Review: "Blackberry Roads" and "The Bridge"
The Georgia Journal: "The Blues Singer"
Free Lunch: "Shadows"
Front Range Review: "Reclamation" and "Slinging a Stone"
Golden Poetry (Legacies Book Publications, 2003): "Waking in a Cabin in the Woods," and "Daybreak"
Haight Ashbury Literary Journal: "Cajones"
ISLE (Interdisciplinary Studies in Literature and Environment), (Oxford University Press): "A Late Spring in Blue Ridge"
the Kerf: "Hiking to Slaughter Gap – November 2002," "Petroglyphs – Rio Grande Gorge" and "Chama"
The Midwest Quarterly: "Old Hippies Come to Happy Hour"
Many Mountains Moving: "Settlement"
Mother Earth Journal: "Independence Day"
The New York Quarterly: "The Commerce Comet" and "Mandelstam"
Pearl: "A-Tisket A-Tasket"

Pinyon: "Climbing Green Mountain" and "Sunday Morning –
   After the Argument"
Poem: "Incan Forest"
Poet Lore: "Carmel-by-the Sea – 8:07 P.M."
Poetry East: "Night Storm" and "Heat Wave"
Rockhurst Review: "One Year"
San Pedro River Review: "Transition Neighborhood" and "The
   Drone Pilot"
Slant: "Whose Woods"
Slipstream: "Oppenheimer"
The South Carolina Review: "Hard Rain"
Southern Indiana Review: "At a Kitchen Table" and "Pantoum for
   Fallujah"
Steam Ticket: "Labor Day – 2005"
Tradeswomen: "A Labor Arbitration"

Anthologies:
*Manifestations – The d'Arts Literary Anthology (DeKalb County
   Council for the Arts, 2004):* "The Blues Singer"
*A Wreath of Poems: Poetry in Cobb County (Lamplighter Books,
   2003):* "Pokeweed" and "A Drop"

Some poems appeared in the chapbook, *The Blues Singer*
published by The Frank Cat Press, 2003. Many thanks to the Editor
Randy Phillis.

Reference in Independence Day to "Born in the U.S.A.," is to the
song written and recorded by Bruce Springsteen; reference to
"This Land is Your Land" is to song written and recorded by
Woody Guthrie

Epigraph in Carmel-by-the Sea from The People of the Abyss, a
book by Jack London (Macmillan, 1903).

Title "A Tisket A Tasket" is taken from a nineteenth century nursery rhyme and has been used as a title in several songs including one written by Al Feldman and Ella Fitzgerald and recorded by Ella Fitzgerald.

Reference in "My Father's Leather Jacket" to "Day-O" is to the traditional Jamaican folk song as recorded by Harry Belafonte.

Reference in "The Last Frontier" to "I'm So Lonesome I Could Cry" is to the song written and recorded by Hank Williams.

Reference in "Shadows" to "Strangers in the Night," is to the song written by Bert Kaempfert, Charles Singleton and Eddie Snyder and recorded by Frank Sinatra.

Reference in "Keeping Count" to "That Old Time Rock and Roll" is to the song written by George Jackson and Thomas E. Jones III and recorded by Bob Seger.

Reference in "Trips" to "Glory Days" is to the song written and recorded by Bruce Springsteen; reference to "The Thrill is Gone," is to the song written by Rick Dannell and Roy Hawkins and recorded by B. B. King.

Reference in "Old Hippies Come to Happy Hour" to "The Weight" is to the song written by Robbie Robertson and recorded by The Band.

Reference in "Nothing Much" to "Jumping Jack Flash" is to the song written by Mick Jagger and Keith Richards and recorded by The Rolling Stones.

Notes

MANDELSTAM
Osip Mandelstam was imprisoned for having written a poem that referred to Joseph Stalin as a "murderer and peasant-slayer." He is believed to have died in 1938. The "Nadia" referred to in the poem is his widow, Nadezhda Mandelstam.

PANTOUM FOR FALLUJAH
Fallujah is a city in Iraq that's history goes back to Babylonian times. It has been the scene of several major battles for control over it since the invasion of Iraq. At various times, it has been under the control of the Iraqi army, Iraqi insurgents, American troops, and ISIL. The events described occurred in 2004 during an American offensive to take control of the city from insurgents.

PLATEAU DU VERCORS
The Plateau du Vercors is a steep, rocky plateau in southeast France that was used as a base by French resisters during World War II. On July 23, 1944, a group of resisters who had been trapped inside caves by German soldiers attempted to escape to the valley. The monument marks the grave of eight who died.

ON A SILENT MORNING
Subcommandante Marcos is a leader of the Zapatista movement in Chiapas, Mexico. Cecilia Rodriquez was a Zapatista spokesperson who was brutally raped by soldiers following her return from a speaking tour in the United States.

About the Author

Michael Walls' poetry has appeared in a variety of literary journals and magazines including *The New York Quarterly, South Carolina Review, Atlanta Review, The Midwest Quarterly, Poetry East, Poet Lore* and others. His award-winning chapbook, *The Blues Singer,* was published by The Frank Cat Press in 2003. His poems and articles have also appeared in law reviews and journals. He is a retired labor lawyer who now spends his time working as a volunteer on environmental issues, hiking, hanging out with friends and family, writing poems and letters to the editor, and listening to rock and roll, blues and jazz. He lives in Atlanta and sometimes in a cabin in the North Georgia mountains.